MAGNA CARTA

THEN AND THERE SERIES

GENERAL EDITOR

MARJORIE REEVES, M.A., Ph.D.

Magna Carta

J. C. HOLT, M.A., D.Phil.

Illustrated from contemporary sources by

H. SCHWARZ

LONGMAN

LONGMAN GROUP LIMITED
London

*Associated companies, branches and representatives
throughout the world*

First published 1961
Ninth impression 1980

ISBN 0 582 20377 5

Acknowledgements

The illustrations appearingon pages 42 and 43,
and 50 and 51 are reproduced by permission
of the Trustees of the British Museum.

*Printed in Hong Kong by
Wilture Enterprises (International) Ltd*

CONTENTS

TO THE READER

THIS book tells the story of a civil war which began in England in 1215, in the time of King John. It is also about the causes and results of this war. Every fact in this book comes from records written at the time the book is describing or from books written by men who lived at this time. These are the original sources to which historians have to go back for their information.

In the same way many of the pictures in this book are based on drawings made by men who lived near this time. Other pictures are of buildings which King John, his friends and his enemies must have known and lived in.

You will find out more about these original sources and pictures by reading pages 78 to 81.

Midsummer 1215

At the end of June 1215 a clerk called Elias of Dereham rode out from King John's court at Windsor. He was an important man who was quite well known, for he was the *steward*[1] of the greatest churchman in the land, Stephen Langton, the Archbishop of Canterbury.

Elias was probably in his thirties. He was to live for another thirty years and before he died he became famous as a builder of churches; he was the man who directed the work on the great new cathedral at Salisbury. But his business in 1215 was not of this kind. In his saddle-bags he carried four *charters*, large *parchment* documents, each bearing the Great *Seal* of King John. These were copies of Magna Carta. He also carried twelve copies of a letter which the King was sending out to his chief local officers, the *sheriffs* of the counties. This letter ordered them to see that the measures contained in Magna Carta were carried out at once.

One of the copies Elias carried was directed to Westmorland, another to Shrop-

[1] You will find the meaning of words printed like *this* in the Glossary on page 86.

I

shire, another to Devon and others to Sussex, Surrey and several southern and midland counties. Elias had a long and tiring ride in front of him. He had to do the whole journey on horseback; there were no mail trains for the delivery of Magna Carta. Probably he got some of the other servants of the Archbishop to help by delivering some of the letters. At all events, three weeks later, he had returned to the King's court, which had moved to Oxford, where he received six more copies of Magna Carta.

Other men, besides Elias, were given copies of Magna Carta and the letters about it, to take to other counties. Some of them were great *barons* or bishops. These documents were thought to be important. Men must have waited for them eagerly throughout the country, hoping that the quarrels of the last few years were ended.

The last few years had seen many troubles both abroad and at home. King John had been at war with King Philip of France and had lost many of his French lands. He had quarrelled bitterly with the Pope, and in 1212 some of his own barons in England had plotted to murder him. The plot had been discovered in time, but the King had not done much since to make people less discontented. The countryside was filled with false rumours. There were stories that the King's reign would soon end. Some were saying that he had been murdered or handed over as a prisoner to his enemies. Others told of attacks on the Queen and young Prince Richard, who were living at Marlborough Castle in Wiltshire. None of these stories was true. Whole villages even believed that robbers were about to attack them and in panic raised the *hue and cry*, only to find that the robbers did not exist.

At last in 1215 something real did happen. In January

some of the King's barons met him at London and demanded reforms. They repeated these demands in the spring and, when John rejected them, made war on him. They marched on London and took the city by surprise. They then forced John to grant them Magna Carta.

So Élias and the other messengers were riding out into a countryside in which a civil war had only just ended. Indeed, in some places battles still continued. At Lincoln, for example, some of the barons were still trying to capture the castle. The charters and letters which Elias and the others carried must have been very welcome news. They meant that there would be peace, that the civil war was at an end. They also meant that the barons had won a great victory over King John. They had made him agree to their demands, saying how he should rule, what he could and could not do.

This was a great achievement. When men wrote about King John in their chronicles, either at the time or later, they nearly always mentioned Magna Carta. Many described it in detail. Some copied it out in full. It was known as the Charter of Liberties. Men quickly came to use it to defend their rights against the King and his officers. Soon they were calling it the Great Charter, in Latin, Magna Carta.

Magna Carta is the most important single document in the history of England. To understand how it came about in 1215, we must first look at King John, at what he was like and at how he ruled, at why men came to hate him and why they demanded Magna Carta from him.

King John

When King John died in 1216 he was buried in Worcester Cathedral where you can see his tomb today. It carries an *effigy* of the King which was made within twenty years of his death. It is made of marble; the nose and crown have been slightly damaged.

King John was a stocky man. When his tomb was opened in 1797 he was found to be 5 ft. 5 ins. tall. He would count as a small man today but was not regarded

Effigy of King John,
Worcester Cathedral

as noticeably small in his own day. He was a determined, energetic, ruthless person who loved hunting, feasting, jewelry and fine clothing. His death was probably brought on by too much eating and drinking, but a week before he died, when he was already sick with his last illness, he was still able to ride thirty miles a day. He liked to have a good time, but he also worked himself very hard.

4

King John insisted that nobody should ignore or invade his rights as King. He was frequently harsh. Sometimes he was cruel. We see this in the way he treated his nephew, Arthur of Brittany. Today, as you can see from this chart, Arthur would have become King of England in 1199 instead of John.

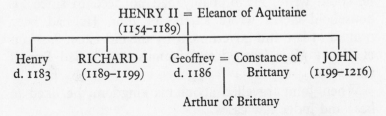

HENRY II = Eleanor of Aquitaine
(1154–1189)

| Henry d. 1183 | RICHARD I (1189–1199) | Geoffrey = Constance of d. 1186 Brittany | JOHN (1199–1216) |

Arthur of Brittany

John managed to get the Crown for himself, but some of Arthur's friends put forward his claim to it. Arthur was thus a possible rival to John and became highly dangerous when he joined in plots and rebellions against his uncle in France. He was captured there in 1202 and imprisoned at Rouen in Normandy. It is probable that he was murdered soon afterwards; some thought that John committed the crime himself. We do not know whether this was so, but at least it must have been done on John's orders.

This crime was not the only one. In 1210 Matilda de Briouze, the wife of one of John's barons, was imprisoned in one of the King's castles, probably Windsor, and starved to death, along with her eldest son, William. We do not know the exact reasons for this. Matilda and her husband, also called William, possibly knew too much about how Arthur of Brittany had died. They had certainly failed to pay the very large debts which they owed the King. William had made war on the King's men, and Matilda had encouraged him. In the end William was outlawed and fled to France, where he died in exile.

5

These are blots on King John's character. But he lived at a time when kings sometimes committed this kind of crime if they considered it worthwhile. There was a good side to John's character as well. He was an educated person who was fond of reading. Sometimes he borrowed books from monastery libraries. We do not know whether he could write. He probably had no need to since his household clerks wrote letters for him. He had been trained in law and government by the old Chief *Justiciar* of Henry II, a learned and famous man called Ranulf Glanville.

When John travelled about his kingdom, he liked to hear and judge law cases.

He often took special care to see that the law was carried out properly and frequently consulted his justices and barons before giving judgement. He could be merciful; for example, when poor people could not pay the fines imposed on them by the justices they were sometimes given a pardon. In this matter of giving justice skilfully and regularly, John was a much better king than his brother Richard the Lion-Heart, for Richard, who was a crusader, was scarcely ever in England and left his ministers to govern for him. Indeed, John maintained the law so well that some said that there had not been such a king since the days of King Arthur.

Richard I, from his seal

But only a few men thought like this. Practically all the history books in John's time were written by clergymen.

Most of these were monks who wrote their books, which they called *chronicles* or *annals*, in monasteries. Before all else, they loved their own order and their own religious house, and most of these men hated King John. He insisted that they should pay special taxes, for many of the monastic orders were very rich. Also, the monks sided

A monk at work on a chronicle

with the Pope in his great quarrel with King John. They quarrelled over who should be chosen as Archbishop of Canterbury and over which of them really should play the biggest part in choosing an archbishop. In 1208, after the dispute had lasted for more than two years, the Pope, whose name was Innocent III, placed England under an *Interdict*. This Interdict lasted until after the King had made his peace with the Pope in 1213. An Interdict meant that all church services ceased, except for baptisms and a sermon in the churchyards on Sundays. Church bells no longer rang. When Matthew Paris, a

Innocent III

7

monk of St. Albans, wrote about this later, he remembered the silence of the bells and drew one with its rope looped in the margin of his chronicle.

King John quickly got his own back. He drove many of the clergy who supported the Pope out of England and seized the lands of many monasteries, putting his own men in charge of them. He gave other monastic lands to his favourite barons. Thus clergymen, especially monks, had reasons of their own for disliking the King and for attacking him in their writings.

Some of those who wrote about the King presented him as a monster, a cruel and greedy tyrant, lazy when he should have been most active, yet sometimes full of the energy of a madman, a man who *scoffed* at religion and who suffered from insane fits of rage. 'Foul as it is, Hell itself is defiled by the fouler presence of John', wrote one of them. Another called him 'Nature's enemy'.

John's treatment of his people, as pictured by Matthew Paris

Most of this was untrue. Many of the stories about John's *brutality* were nothing but inventions. Writers repeated the worst gossip about the King as monks exchanged their news or as travellers carried it from one monastery to another. John was not a pious man, like his son, Henry III, but he certainly did not hate religion and the Church, as some writers said. For example, he made devout gifts to various churches and gave *alms* to the poor at Christmas, Easter and other festivals. He encouraged men to give money to Hugh of Avalon, Bishop of Lincoln, to help build the great new choir at Lincoln cathedral. He was especially fond of the church of Worcester and of its two bishops who had been made saints, St. Oswald and St. Wulfstan. St. Wulfstan was John's patron saint. If you turn back to the picture of the King's effigy on page 4 you will see that the two saints appear on it, one to each side of the King's head.

However, although most of the stories of the monks were untrue, men were still ready to listen to them. John was unpopular not only with the Church, but also with many barons and knights and with some of the townsfolk. Also, although he was clever and energetic, he failed to live up to what men thought a king should be, because he gave in too often. He lost most of his lands in France to King Philip of France. When he made up his quarrel with the Pope he surrendered his kingdom to the Pope and received it back again as the Pope's *vassal*. In 1215 he gave in to the barons' demands for Magna Carta. His reign ended in a bitter civil war. After his death most men were prepared to believe the worst of him. In their eyes he was a bad king.

This judgement was unfair. To understand this we must look at what he was trying to do.

9

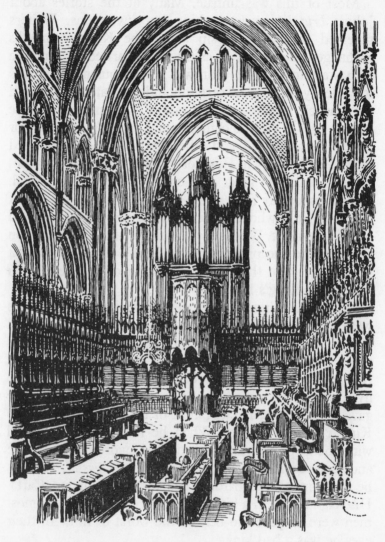

Lincoln Cathedral: St. Hugh's Choir. The organ and stalls were put there much later

King John, his brother, King Richard the Lion-Heart, and his father, King Henry II, ruled over other lands besides England. These included the whole of western France, from Normandy and Brittany south to the county of Anjou and the enormous duchy of Aquitaine, which included Poitou and Gascony. They held these lands as vassals of the kings of France. Indeed, they controlled more of France than the kings of France did, and the French kings naturally objected to vassals who were more powerful than themselves. Henry II tried to get more lands in France, but he was not very successful in the end, for he had to pay more attention as time passed to defending what he already had. Richard the Lion-Heart had to fight especially hard to hold the frontiers of Normandy against the French. In 1196 he built a great new castle called Château Gaillard just inside the borders of Normandy at a place called Les Andelys on the banks of the river Seine. This is what it looks like today.

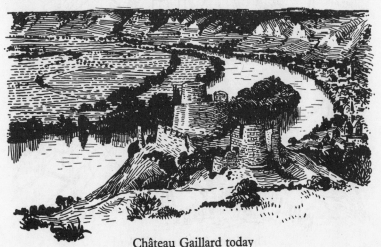

Château Gaillard today

The French finally seized many of these lands in the reign of King John. In 1204 they captured Château Gaillard and conquered the duchy of Normandy. In the

The siege of Château Gaillard

next year they captured most of the English garrisons further south in Anjou and Touraine. John's rule had been driven back to Poitou and Gascony. You can see the extent of his loss from this map.

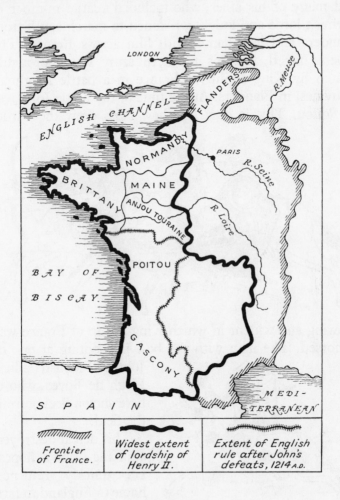

| Frontier of France. | Widest extent of lordship of Henry II. | Extent of English rule after John's defeats, 1214 A.D. |

John tried to fight back. He spent ten years collecting the money to pay for a huge army and preparing his allies for a great attack on the French. In 1214 he took an army to Poitou, while his half-brother, William of Salisbury, and many of his allies, who included a large number of Flemish lords and knights, planned to march south from Flanders and join hands with him across France. The scheme failed, for this northern army was thoroughly beaten by King Philip of France in a battle fought at Bouvines, in Flanders. At the time of the battle John was in Poitou. This is how Matthew Paris drew the battle,

showing an incident in which King Philip of France was unhorsed. The man with the bow is shooting at one of

John's Flemish allies, Hugh de Boves, who is here shown fleeing from the field.

This defeat destroyed all King John's hopes. He quickly returned home to England to face his angry barons. Many of them considered him a failure, for he had not succeeded in holding Normandy in 1204, and now, in 1214, his grand plan for recovering the lost lands had been defeated. King John's wars were not all failures. But John had failed in the chief war he was fighting, and hence men felt that he had failed in one of the main duties of a medieval king. This was a time when men admired good knights, especially when they fought in the service of God on the Crusade. Knighthood was an ideal. This is illustrated, for example, in this beautiful picture of a knight drawn by Matthew Paris.

A knight of the thirteenth century

But the defeat was not mainly John's fault. It was very difficult to defend Normandy and his other French possessions. Henry II and Richard the Lion-Heart had, in the end, only just been able to hold their own. King Philip of France became increasingly strong, while the English kings fought a losing battle against the difficulties of defending such a long frontier line and controlling such a large empire.

The barons wanted it both ways. They blamed John for failing in war. But they themselves were not very willing to help pay the costs of war. They complained that the King was ruling too harshly and too strictly, and was taxing them heavily in various ways. John had to do this because he needed the money to hire troops, build and repair castles, pay his allies on the Continent and generally conduct the war against the French. Richard the Lion-Heart and Henry II had ruled in very much the same way. John frequently copied what his father and brother had done. Indeed, he made a point of saying so in his quarrel with the barons in 1215. But one extra difficulty he had was that prices kept going up and he had to pay more for his soldiers and for their food and equipment than his father and brother had done

HOW TO DECIDE ABOUT KING JOHN

Sometimes King John was cruel, but sometimes, too, he was merciful to poor men and people in distress. He liked to judge people and saw that men observed the law.

The monks who wrote about him said that he was a tyrant, but they had special reasons for hating him.

He lost many of his lands in France, but it was becoming less and less easy to hold on to them.

What do you think about him?

King John and his Kingdom

King John was an energetic and active ruler who travelled restlessly about his kingdom. He rarely stayed in one place for more than a week or so at a time. London and Westminster were not then the centre of government as they are today. The centre of government was where the King was as he moved about the country. At any one time King John might be at some great royal castle, at Corfe, for example, or Windsor, or Newcastle-on-Tyne;

Corfe Castle today

17

or at a hunting lodge, perhaps Clarendon, near Salisbury, or Clipstone, in Sherwood Forest; or at his palace of Westminster; or at a castle or hall in one of the great towns of his kingdom, at Winchester, for example, or at Oxford, Northampton, Lincoln or York.

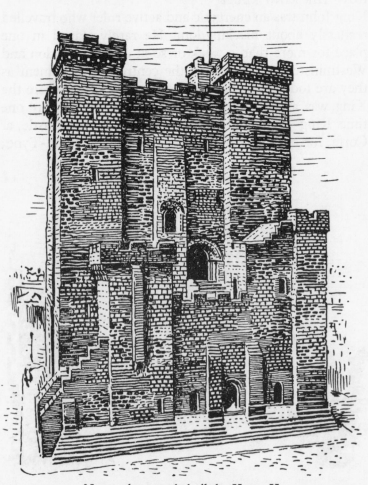

Newcastle: a castle built by Henry II

Oxford Castle

John even travelled once a year or so through the northern counties of Northumberland, Westmorland and Cumberland and often made this journey in midwinter. At this time of the year it must have been a cold and wearisome trip, for the King and his companions travelled on horseback, and his goods and all the things necessary for carrying on the government, quills and ink, parchment and wax, tables and chairs, barrels full of money and parcels packed with documents, were carried on pack-horses or in carts. King John knew England better than either Richard the Lion-Heart, his brother, or Henry II, his father, had done, for both these kings spent much time abroad. Richard was scarcely ever in England, and never, for example, visited the northern counties, except for one single journey as far as Nottingham.

King John travelled about like this, sometimes in order to visit his own estates, just as the Queen today visits Sandringham and Balmoral, sometimes to hunt in one of the many royal forests, sometimes to fight against the

Riding off to hunt

Welsh or the Scots, sometimes to deal with troubles in different parts of his kingdom. Also, to travel about like this was the proper way to govern. On his journeys the King met and talked to his barons, the great bishops and other important people, often entertaining them at a feast in some great royal castle or manor house, and often being entertained by them. As he travelled, too, the King was able to keep an eye on his officials, especially his sheriffs and *bailiffs*, who were in charge of his local government. Sometimes these men were lazy; sometimes they were bribed by local men so that they did not do their job properly; sometimes they helped themselves to money which really belonged to the King. On these journeys King John also judged legal quarrels between his subjects; frequently he collected fines and taxes; sometimes he asked searching questions about the services due to him and ordered that they should be increased. John's restless movements brought the King's government home to people more than ever before.

Some men got what they wanted from royal visits of this kind. Often powerful men were able to obtain the King's confirmation of their privileges, or perhaps get some new favour from him. Others, even sometimes poor people, might be able to appeal to the King against the harshness of his sheriffs or his barons. But on the whole men hated these regular inspections. The poor might be taxed; rich and powerful men, both barons and church-men, might have to pay heavily for favours they wanted and might be punished severely for breaking the law. In 1206, for example, when the King visited Lancashire, he demanded that the Abbot of Furness should pay over £300 for ignoring the forest laws which protected the royal rights of hunting. In maintaining the law as he went about the country, the King was also preserving his own rights over his barons and his people. Many men would have preferred the King to leave them alone to fight out their own quarrels. In their eyes John interfered too much.

Also, the King's journeys were a burden in themselves. When he and his men lodged in towns, the whole town was called upon to lodge and feed them, and the chief men of the town were required to entertain the King with feasting. When the men of York failed to welcome him and his men properly in 1201 they had to pay nearly £70 to avoid the King's wrath. As he travelled about the country, fodder was needed for the pack-horses and chargers, carts might have to be hired, corn might have to be taken for the King's use. Sometimes his men paid for these things, but sometimes not. In either case these demands were usually heavy and disturbed the settled life of the countryside.

THE KING AND THE LAW

Today the government has to obey a large number of laws and other rules which did not exist in John's time. If, for example, the police imprison you today, they can be compelled to bring you before a magistrate within a day or so to show why they have arrested you. If they cannot show good reason, you will be freed. In John's time this was not so. Then a sheriff could hold his prisoners for many months, perhaps for years, before the King's justices came to listen to cases. Sometimes they came round only because the prisons were filled to overflowing. If the King himself ordered someone to be imprisoned, then no one could free him without the King's permission.

Again, today, if you are convicted for a crime, the

magistrate or judge can only impose the statutory penalty and no more, that is the punishment laid down by Act of Parliament for the particular crime. In John's time, especially in the case of barons, things were quite different. If a baron committed a crime, even if it were just a matter of some small offence against the forest law or of failing to appear before the justices when he was summoned, he could be placed in the King's 'mercy'. He would then be compelled to pay for the King's 'grace' or good will, and the King frequently fixed a very high price for it. Sometimes these fines were far bigger than the sum a baron could really afford to pay, and, as a result, could only be paid off after many years of borrowing and scraping.

Besides this, the King had great power over the lands and families of his barons. For example, when a baron died, his son had to pay a sum of money in order to succeed to his father's lands. This payment was called a *relief*. At this time men were coming to think that no one should be compelled to pay more than £100 as a relief, but, in fact, there was no law enforcing this, and the King frequently asked for enormous sums. For example, when a baron called John de Lacy succeeded to the land of his

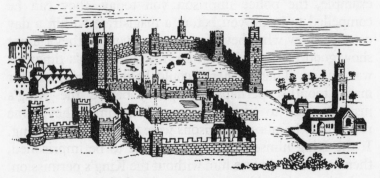

Pontefract in the seventeenth century

Clitheroe today

father, Roger, in 1213, he had to promise a huge relief of more than £4,500. It is no wonder that John de Lacy, who was a great landlord with castles at Pontefract, in Yorkshire, and Clitheroe, in Lancashire, joined the rebellion against the King in 1215 and supported Magna Carta.

These are just a few of the ways in which important matters were settled as the King wished and not, as in our time, as the law demanded. There were many others. However, it would not be true to say that there was no such thing as law in John's time, and that his command or smallest whim could settle anything and everything. There were many laws saying, for example, how men should settle disputes between each other, how robbers and murderers should be accused and punished, or how

23

the courts of law should be conducted. But there were few laws which clearly stated how the King should behave towards his people, even towards his barons. Everybody, including the King himself, agreed that he had to govern justly and protect his subjects and the Church. Indeed, John, like other English kings, swore a solemn oath that he would do all this during the ceremony of his coronation at Westminster in 1199, just as Queen Elizabeth II swore to do the same at her coronation in 1953. The trouble was that King John, like other English kings before him, was left to decide just what this promise meant.

The King was the fount of justice. He could give judgement so as to favour his friends and to spite those whom he disliked. In 1201, for example, he encouraged one of his sheriffs, William de Stuteville, to claim the lands of a great Yorkshire baron called William de Mowbray. William de Mowbray offered to pay the King over £1,300 to be treated justly according to the law of England. Nevertheless, when the King heard the case at York, he judged that Mowbray should surrender part of his lands to de Stuteville. Needless to say, William de Stuteville also had offered the King a large sum of money for a favourable judgement. Despite the fact that the case went against de Mowbray, the King still insisted that he should pay the enormous sum he had offered. He was still paying it off in instalments in 1215. By then he had joined the rebels against the King.

The King could only punish one of his barons after he had been judged guilty by a court. But such a court, which might consist of the barons who were the King's special friends or of the Barons of the *Exchequer*, whose chief job was to collect taxes and debts due to the King, often did just what the King wanted. In 1205, for example, a well-known Lincolnshire knight called Thomas of Moulton offered the King a large sum of money to be made Sheriff of Lincolnshire. The King accepted this and agreed with Thomas that he would not take this office from him except by the judgement of a court. In 1208, when he had fallen behind in paying his debts to the King and had also come into his displeasure in other ways, Thomas was deprived of his office, heavily fined and imprisoned in Rochester Castle. The King ordered that he was not to be freed until he had paid all his debts to the last penny. Before he was sent to Rochester Thomas was in the hands of the Barons of the Exchequer: they, most probably, had decided what his fate should be. Thomas had got his judgement in a court, but it had not done him any good. He, too, rebelled against the King in 1215.

King John did not break the law when he did this kind of thing so much as twist it to his own ends. A king also had the power to add to and change the law, so long as he did it with the advice of his barons and other great men of the land. In some ways this limited what he could do; he had no power, for example, to take a general tax from his barons unless they agreed, and John never tried to do so without their agreement. But there was no law stating that the King should consult all the great men of the land before he decided something important, and there was no law saying where and how these men should be called together to give the King their advice or agree to his plans. No doubt, on some occasions, King John just consulted those barons and bishops with whom he was friendly. On other occasions he summoned larger gatherings. Sometimes, but only rarely, such a meeting opposed his wishes.

However, in 1215 there was no such thing as Parliament. In those days the King was held in check, not by Parliament but by the fact that if he treated too many of his barons and the rest of his people too harshly, then they would rebel against him. This is just what John did by 1215. He tried to prevent rebellion by demanding *hostages* from those barons whom he suspected were ready to take sides against him. Often these hostages were the barons' sons and daughters, and so the King could threaten that he would punish the children, and perhaps even kill them, if their fathers rebelled. In the end even taking hostages was no use. John's actions convinced many men that the enormous personal powers of the King should be subject to agreed rules and regulations, and they so distrusted and hated him that they were ready to rebel and fight for this.

SOME OF THOSE WHO REBELLED AGAINST THE KING

Many of those who rebelled against King John had been treated harshly by him, like John de Lacy or William de

Mowbray or Thomas of Moulton, and felt that they had personal wrongs to avenge. In the end many powerful men joined together against him, like Richard of Clare, Earl of Hertford, or Robert de Vere, Earl of Oxford, who had a great castle at Hedingham, in Essex, or Roger Bigod, Earl of Norfolk, who had just built a

Richard of Clare, from his seal

Castle Hedingham today

Framlingham Castle

remarkably strong castle at Framlingham in Suffolk. But you must not imagine that these men had all the right on their side or that they were specially brave and heroic in rebelling in this way. Some of them were very half-hearted in their rebellion and had earlier been quite friendly with the King. Some, too, behaved just as badly towards others as the King did towards them. Some rebelled just to suit their own ends, some simply because they liked a good fight.

A baron called Robert de Ros shows us what these men were like. Robert came from the north of England, where he held the important castle of Wark - on - Tweed, in Northumberland, and another castle at Helmsley, in Yorkshire, where he

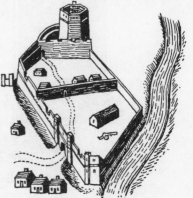

Wark Castle as it was in Elizabeth I's reign

had just rebuilt the keep. He was an important and wealthy man who had married one of the daughters of William the Lion, King of Scotland. In 1215 he was in his early forties.

Like many others, he suffered harsh treatment occasionally at the hands of King John and also earlier still in the reign of King Richard. He had to

William the Lion, from his seal

28

pay nearly £700 in 1190 for the baronies he *inherited* from his father, and over £300 in 1205 for the land he inherited through his mother. In 1196 he allowed a French knight who was in his hands as a prisoner to escape from his charge, and had to pay £800 as a punishment. In 1207 he allowed another prisoner to escape—this time a man who was accused of murder—and had to pay £200 to avoid the King's wrath. Robert was careless in guarding prisoners. At times, too, King John was doubtful of his

The *keep* at Helmsley today

loyalty. In 1205 he seized Robert's lands for a time and gave them back only on condition that Robert surrendered one of his sons as a hostage for his loyalty.

We might imagine from this that Robert was one of the King's most bitter enemies, but this was far from being so. In fact he was a close acquaintance of the King and was often with the court as it moved about the country. Sometimes he partnered the King in the gambling games John and his friends played after dinner. He was made Sheriff of Cumberland in 1213 and stayed loyal to King John until only a few weeks before the King granted Magna Carta. Robert took a long time to make up his mind before rebelling.

29

Robert was a very religious man. He was a descendant of the Yorkshire baron, Walter Espec, who had founded Rievaulx Abbey, and Robert himself made many gifts to this abbey. He also founded a hospital for lepers at Bolton in Northumberland and, just before he died, joined the order of the Knights Templar. We might feel from this that he joined the rebellion against King John from a feeling that the rebel barons' demands were right and just; that he was inspired, if you like, by ideals and principles. But, when he had the chance, Robert was almost as ruthless and self-seeking as King John. During the civil war which followed Magna Carta, he was quick to rob weaker men of their lands. Long afterwards, in 1220, when the Sheriff of Yorkshire tried to restore his lands to one of these men Robert had turned out, Robert's men attacked the sheriff's bailiffs with bows and arrows, wounded some of them and put them to flight.

There were others like Robert de Ros. The leader of the barons in 1215 was a man called Robert fitz Walter, whose chief estates were at Dunmow in Essex and Baynard Castle in London. Robert, at least, had no cause to sneer at his King's disastrous wars in France, for in 1203 he had been in charge of the castle at Vaudreuil, near Château Gaillard, in Normandy, and had surrendered it to the French without a serious fight. The rebel barons now gave Robert the high-sounding title of 'Marshal of the Army of God and Holy Church'. But he had, in fact, persecuted at least two churches for he had quarrelled with the monks of St. Albans and of the Priory of Binham in Norfolk. In the end the quarrel was settled in the King's court, but not before Robert fitz Walter had surrounded Binham Priory with his men, in an attempt to starve out the monks. King John's enforcement of the law in this case was probably one of the reasons why Robert rebelled. He was one of those who plotted to have the King murdered in 1212.

You can see from this that the barons who rebelled against King John were a very mixed bag. They wanted to make the King rule according to law. But they were also ready to break or ignore the law themselves, and to use force in order to look after their own interests.

SOME OF THOSE WHO WERE ON THE KING'S SIDE

Only a small number of people rebelled against King John in 1215. The peasants, who formed the greater part of the population, took no part in the rebellion at all. Some of the townspeople and merchants were on the King's side. Not even all the great barons and the knights rose against the King. In fact, the greatest barons of all, the earls, were about evenly divided between the two sides.

The strongest support for the King naturally came from the sheriffs and the men in charge of his castles, who were usually called *constables*. Some of these sheriffs and constables were also barons, but some of them were important only because of the position which the King had given them. Sometimes they behaved rather like the story-book evil sheriff in the *ballads* of Robin Hood. Some of them were foreigners whom the King had brought back to England from Normandy and Poitou. These men were especially hated. One of the most important of them was called Faulkes de Breauté. During the civil war he became one of John's chief generals and sheriff of several counties in the southern midlands. He was a great enemy of the monks of St. Albans and did them much harm. Stories were told that he dreamed of a stone falling on him

from the roof of the Abbey as a punishment from St. Alban for his robbing of the monks; this frightened him and, as a result, the story goes, he made apologies to the monks, but did not return his loot. This is a picture which Matthew Paris drew to illustrate this story. You can see that he drew the stone very big and that he disliked Faulkes very much.

Many others shared Matthew's feelings about Faulkes. Faulkes lived on in England after the civil war. But he quickly lost his old influence and many of the castles and offices he had held. In the end, in 1224, some of his relatives and men rebelled in Bedford Castle. Faulkes fled abroad, never to return, but this is what happened to those who were captured when Bedford Castle was taken.

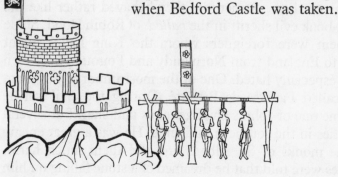

The effigy of
William of Salisbury
in
Salisbury Cathedral

Not all the King's supporters were like Faulkes. Some were members of the royal family, like William, Earl of Salisbury, John's half-brother, whose effigy you can still see in Salisbury Cathedral. Others were bishops who owed their promotion to the King and stood by him loyally. In the picture below Matthew Paris shows one of these, Peter des Roches, Bishop of Winchester, with the Earl of Pembroke and another bishop, as they stood on the shore at Sandwich, in Kent, watching a battle at sea towards the end of the civil war. The two bishops are blessing the English sailors. Other supporters of the King were great barons, like Ranulf, Earl of Chester, one of the greatest men in northern England and along the Welsh border. John took great care to keep him on his side, and Ranulf was rewarded with the earldom of Lincoln for his loyal support during the civil war. Later, men wrote ballads about him as the Good Earl Randle.

The most interesting of these men on the King's side was also the most respected of the English barons. This was William Marshal, Earl of Pembroke. William was nearly seventy years old in 1215. His memories went back

Watching the
battle of Sandwich

33

to the troublesome reign of King Stephen, when he had been surrendered by his father as a hostage to the King. He had quickly endeared himself to Stephen, among other things by challenging him and beating him at a game of jackstraw, which is still played today and is rather like 'conkers'. This was when William was six years old at the most, and at a time when his life was in danger for King Stephen could have killed him as a result of his father's treachery. Since then William had established a great reputation as a brave and loyal knight who had served King Henry II, his eldest son Henry, King Richard and King John, in turn. William had several quarrels with John and even had to surrender hostages to him. But he never deserted the King's cause, for he would

have thought it an act of unpardonable disloyalty to rebel against his lord. Moreover, when John was dead, William stood by his son, the boy King Henry III, and helped to establish him as king with the support of Ranulf of Chester and other barons. William had many estates. The chief ones were in Ireland and in Wales, where he had built the fine *keep* at Pembroke Castle and where he was a great power among the

The keep at Pembroke

turbulent barons of the

34

Welsh *Marches*. When he died in 1219 he was buried in the Temple Church at London. There is a fine effigy of an old man in this church, which was damaged by bombing in the last war. Some experts think that this represents William Marshal. The head looks like this.

The effigy in the Temple Church, London

William looked after himself well enough. When Normandy was lost in 1204 he managed to keep his own lands there by doing *homage* to the French king, Philip; this greatly annoyed King John. In 1215, while William remained loyal to the King, his eldest son joined the rebels; one of them was certain to be on the winning side. William was not only loyal and chivalrous, he was also very successful. Sometimes he was able to have it both ways. Men admired him, not just because he was an example of what a knight should be, but also because he had made his chivalry and loyalty pay. From a poor landless *squire* he had become Earl Marshal of England, and had done so in a way which men respected. In him, John had a powerful ally.

The Rebellion against King John

The barons who rebelled in 1215 had been scheming against King John for a long time. In 1212 some of them had joined in a plot to murder him. This had been discovered and had failed. In 1213 they began to demand that the King should restore what they called their 'ancient liberties'. Soon they were asking that John

The coronation of Henry I, drawn by Matthew Paris

should accept the rules contained in a charter of liberties in which King Henry I had made promises of good government and fair treatment at his coronation in 1100. Some of them banded together and swore an *oath* that they would fight to the death to force the King to do this. The chroniclers of St. Albans tell of two such oaths, one made at St. Paul's Cathedral, London, in August 1213 and another made at the Abbey of Bury St. Edmunds in November 1214.

These demands were placed before the King on several occasions in 1213, 1214 and the early months of 1215. In the talks which followed, one man was especially important. This was Stephen Langton, the Archbishop of Canterbury, who had come to England in 1213 when John made his peace with the Pope. Stephen was present at all the discussions; he tried to get the barons to be moderate and reasonable in their demands, and he tried to persuade the King to accept these demands in good faith. He wanted to settle the quarrel by a peaceful agreement and to avoid civil war. There is no effigy of the Archbishop, but this is what his seal looked like. It is a particularly beautiful one.

Stephen Langton's seal

King John was unwilling to accept the barons' demands. However, rather than refuse them outright, he tried to put them off and cause delays so that he could get ready to fight. By the early months of 1215 he was busy preparing for a civil war. His men were fortifying his castles, replenishing supplies, bringing in bolts for the garrisons' cross-bows, salting down meat to feed them in case of long sieges, and storing corn to make bread and feed the horses. The King was also bringing soldiers over from parts of France and Flanders where he still had friends.

At the end of April 1215 the barons met in arms at Stamford. They marched to Brackley, where they sent their final demands to the King. When the King rejected these they declared war by withdrawing their allegiance. The war which followed was soon over. On May 17th the barons took London by surprise, with the help of some of the citizens. They quickly put the city in a state of defence, repairing the walls where necessary. This was a disaster for the King, for London was the chief city of the land, and he decided at once that he would have to make peace.

Stephen Langton now went to and fro, carrying the barons' demands to the King at Windsor and the King's promises and offers to the rebels at London. It was only after a fortnight had passed in this way that an agreement on the terms of peace seemed possible. It was then arranged that there should be a great meeting of the barons and the King in a meadow between Staines and Windsor on June 15th.

The journey from London to Windsor in 1215 was through open country, not as it is today through busy streets and suburbs. As the barons rode west from the city to meet the King they would already be among fields and farmland as they passed the royal palace and the great abbey at Westminster. Their journey took them as far as Staines, which lies on the north bank of the River Thames in Middlesex. Here an old Roman road to Silchester crossed the river. As Windsor lay upstream on the south bank of the river, the barons still had the river crossing as a line of defence against any possible attack by the King. North of the Thames, Staines was protected against approach from the west by the marshy valley of the River Colne. It was an excellent position for the barons' purposes. They were taking no unnecessary chances.

This little town of Staines was the nearest place of any importance to the King's castle at Windsor. On the night of June 14th, 1215, it must have been crowded with the great company of barons and their followers. Early the following morning they rode out across the bridge and then westwards up the river to meet the King and his advisors in the meadow of Staines, or, as some men called it, Runnymede. This was a large meadow, triangular in shape, a mile long and half a mile across at its widest point. The north and longest side was bounded by the Thames. To the south-west its limit was fixed by an old river-bed in which the Thames once flowed, and which still carries water. Beyond this, to the west and south-west lay a low range of hills, culminating in Cooper's Hill, from which a stream flowed down continuing the southern boundary of the meadow to the east and then north to the Thames. The whole of this area was very low lying and was frequently flooded, so much so that a causeway was built some years later from the neighbouring village of Egham to Staines. Runnymede at any time was almost an island, only to be reached from Staines across the little stream or down the bank of the Thames from Windsor.

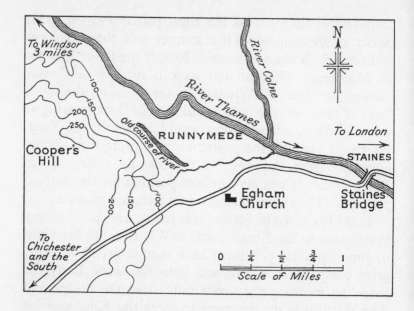

In wet weather, when the Thames was flooded, its waters probably spread into the old river-bed and flowed through to the course of the little stream, thus forming a proper island. This is what it had been centuries earlier when it was named by the Anglo-Saxons. The name meant 'the meadow of the assembly island'. It was a meeting place where, in times past, men had met to discuss public business.

King John and his rebel barons first met in this place on June 15th. It must have been a large gathering numbering hundreds of men. They continued to meet daily at Runnymede for a week or more. We do not know exactly what happened on each of these days; we do not know how the meetings were conducted. As far as we know, none of the men who later wrote about Magna Carta were eye-witnesses of the scene at Runnymede.

There were no newspaper reporters present, no radio or television broadcasts, as there would certainly be at an important modern conference. In spite of this, we know that two days during the week at Runnymede were especially important. The first was the first day of the meeting, June 15th. The second was four days later, June 19th. We can find out some of the things which happened on these two days.

On the first day, June 15th, the King and the rebels formally and publicly agreed to preliminary terms of peace, leaving some details and problems for further discussion. You can read these terms in a document known as the Articles of the Barons. It is written in Latin and is quite a long document. It measures $21\frac{3}{4}$ in. long by $10\frac{1}{2}$ in. wide and is closely written in small writing. If you visit the British Museum at London you can see it. There is a picture of a portion of it on pages 42 and 43.

Runnymede from the south-west

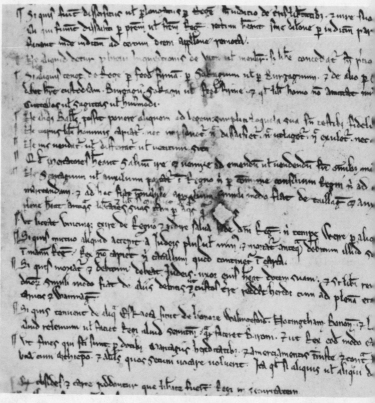

A portion of

This document still left many things undone. Parts of it needed discussing further. Some sections did not seem quite right to the King. Some sections did not seem quite right to the rebels. Some sections had been deliberately left vague for the moment so that they could be settled later. So we may imagine that there was much coming and going during the next few days. There must have been many meetings, sometimes of small groups, sometimes of large, to discuss this or that point. Many suggestions for improving and adding to the terms of peace must have been made. Also, the King and the rebel barons had to agree on how the terms were to be carried out. The barons wanted more than the King's promise; they wanted a good guarantee that the terms would not be forgotten, ignored or broken; they wanted to see that the King's sheriffs applied them properly throughout the country. The King also wanted something. If he was agreeing to the barons' demands he wanted a proper

43

return to peace; he wanted to be able to collect his rents and taxes once again; he wanted especially to get back London, the greatest and most prosperous city of the land, which the rebels had taken from him. He and the barons, therefore, had to talk and argue about this too.

By June 19th all this was done. There must then have been another large gathering like that four days earlier. In this several things happened. The rebels became once again men of King John. At the beginning of the civil war they had defied him by withdrawing their allegiance from him. They now had to renew their oaths of loyalty and each one present knelt down before him, placing his hands between the hands of the King, and accepted him as lord. This was doing their homage to him once again. The King also formally granted to the barons the terms of peace which had been worked out over the last four days. Indeed, he and his opponents, and probably his chief advisers too, gave a solemn oath that they would accept these terms in good faith. The Archbishop and the bishops who were present witnessed all this. They also agreed that they would put their seals to a fair copy of the terms, so that they should not be altered or changed in any way. By these acts two important things were brought about. First, a firm peace was once more established in the realm of England. Secondly, the terms which the barons had obtained became part of the law of the land.

On this same day several other things were done. Letters were being made ready to send to King's sheriffs and those who held his castles letting them know of the peace and ordering them to stop making war on the King's opponents. The letters with which Elias of Dereham set out on his journeys were also being prepared. Lastly arrangements were made about London. It was agreed that the barons should continue to hold the city until August 15th. This was as a pledge that the King would carry out his promises by that date. This agreement was written down in a separate treaty. You can see the King's copy of it in the museum of the Public Record Office at London.

While this was being done the King's clerks were producing proper copies of the terms of peace in the form of charters. Seven of them had been done by June 23rd, when Elias of Dereham and other messengers received them. The clerks of the King's household, on whom this work of writing fell, must have been very busy doing all this copying. It probably took one man most of a day to produce one well-written copy of Magna Carta.

The meeting at Runnymede did not end on June 19th. Some men were waiting for the copies of Magna Carta or the letters which they had to take. Others had personal demands and requests to put before the King. Magna Carta stated that King John was to restore property and possessions which he had seized unlawfully. Those present who felt they had suffered injustice in this way, now demanded that the King should do as he had promised. For nearly a week the King was compelled to listen to these complaints. He had to satisfy many of them by ordering his men to restore what was claimed, sometimes land, sometimes castles, sometimes the right to hold a market and fair, for example. He also had to restore the sons and daughters of some of the barons, whom his men held as hostages for the good behaviour of their parents.

All this kept both the King and the barons very busy. He still visited Runnymede daily up to June 23rd, and stayed at Windsor until the night of the 25th, when he moved to Winchester. Even then some of the claims which had been brought against him had not yet been settled. Some of these were very important. One baron, for example, was asking to have charge of the Tower of London. Another was claiming the castle of York. These were big demands. John was very unwilling to accept them. These and other matters were put off for later discussion.

So the agreement at Runnymede was not complete. There were still points on which the King and barons might quarrel. As a result distrust and suspicion between them increased in the summer months and led in the autumn to a new civil war.

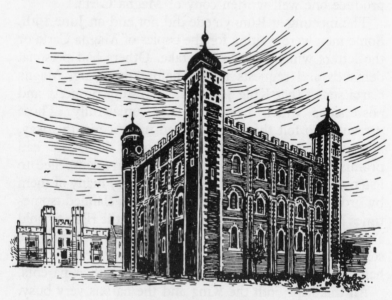

The Tower of London

Magna Carta

At least thirteen copies of Magna Carta were written out by the King's clerks in the summer of 1215. There were almost certainly more, probably one for each sheriff. Only four of these copies exist today. You can still see the one which was sent to Lincolnshire in the cathedral at Lincoln. There is another copy in Salisbury Cathedral. There are two which you can see at the British Museum at London, but one of them has been badly damaged by a fire which occurred in 1731. With this exception, they are all large, handsome documents of parchment. They are written in Latin, neatly and clearly. The Lincoln copy measures $18\frac{1}{2}$ in. by $17\frac{3}{4}$ in. The undamaged copy in the British museum measures $20\frac{1}{4}$ in. by $13\frac{1}{2}$ in. You can see what this last one looks like in the reproduction on pages 50 and 51.

All these copies have now been spoilt in one respect. In 1215 they all carried a wax impression of the King's Great Seal. This hung from the bottom of the documents by a tag of parchment passing through a slit, or by silken cords which passed through holes. It carried on the one side an impression of the King in majesty, enthroned with crown, sword and sceptre. On the other side he was represented in armour on horseback. King John's seal measured $3\frac{5}{8}$ in. across, and one side of it is shown on the front cover of this book. The other side is shown on page 48.

King John's Great Seal,
the reverse side

On the damaged copy of the charter in the British Museum the wax of the seal has melted to a shapeless blob. It has been removed from the other three.

These documents were sealed to show that they came from the King and that they had been drawn up by his order. They were royal acts. King John did not sign Magna Carta.

We do not possess the signature of any English king before Edward III. Just as we sign documents today, so men attached the impressions of their seals to them in John's time. But the King would not even do this. The *matrix* of the Great Seal, from which the wax impressions were made, was kept by the *Chancellor*. Documents were sealed by one of the Chancellor's clerks, who was called the *Spigurnel*.

Magna Carta was an agreement between the King and his barons at the end of a civil war. In its form, however, it was not a peace *treaty*. Kings made such treaties with other kings. But kings did not make treaties with their subjects. They were not their equals. Therefore, the agreement in 1215 took the form of a gracious act by the King. John granted privileges and rights to his subjects. He had been compelled to do this by a rebellion. But he was not going to admit this publicly. He now made this grant, as Magna Carta stated, 'for the safety of our soul and the souls of our *ancestors* and *heirs*, for the honour of God and the exaltation of Holy Church and the reform of our kingdom.'

This grant was recorded in a charter. This kind of document was in daily use at this time. It was used by the King and by barons, bishops, abbots and knights to grant land or rights and privileges. What Magna Carta contained was new and tremendously important. But, as a document, its form was commonplace.

These first charters were written without any divisions into chapters or paragraphs. Historians have found it convenient to divide the document up into sixty-three short sections or chapters. You can see from this that it contains a lot of regulations. For a medieval charter, it was very lengthy indeed.

WHAT MAGNA CARTA SAID: I. *For the Barons*

The most important of King John's opponents were the barons, and Magna Carta was drawn up chiefly to meet their demands. These demands were aimed, in the first place, at preserving and strengthening their positions as barons.

Most of the barons were great landowners and held vast estates which were often scattered through several counties. They were tenants of the King and held these lands of him in return for performing certain services.

The most important of these was a military one. The barons, at their own expense, had to send the King a number of knights whenever he was engaged in war. The number of these knights was fixed for each baron and might vary, from one or two to a hundred or more. William de Mowbray, for example, owed the King the service of eighty-one knights; Robert de Ros, the service of fourteen. The barons also had to help the King in other ways, especially by giving him aid in the form of money on certain recognized occasions, as when he

Magna Carta, the copy in the Britis[h]

knighted his eldest son, or, if they agreed, on exceptional occasions when he could show some urgent need for help.

In addition to this the King had certain rights over his barons, their families and their lands. When a baron died, his heir had to pay a sum of money which was called a relief, in order to succeed to his lands, which were called a *barony*. If the heir was under age he became a royal *ward*, and the King could take all the income and the profits of the barony until the ward was twenty-one, or he might grant them, with the ward, as a special favour to one of his friends. If the baron left a widow, then she could not marry again without the King's consent; if she was wealthy and held large estates, the King would often compel her to marry someone of his own choosing. The same might happen if a baron left one or more daughters. Sometimes the King sold such marriages to the highest bidder.

These baronial duties and royal rights were one of the biggest causes of the quarrel between King John and his barons in 1215. Some of them had become out of date. For example, if all the knights whose service was owned by the barons had been called together at the same time, they would have formed a large army of about five thousand men. But they were only bound to serve for a period of forty days, and such an army was thus quite useless for the long campaigns which Henry II, Richard, and John had to fight in France. It was costly to transport across the Channel, and by the time it was mustered in the field, in Normandy for example, the forty-day limit had almost been reached when the knights could return home. What these three kings often did, therefore, was to ask for money instead of knights and then use it to hire soldiers for longer periods. Some of these were usually barons and knights, some Welsh archers, some crossbow-men and men-at-arms from Flanders and the Low Countries. This money was often collected as a general tax which was called *scutage* and was charged against the barons at so much, perhaps £1 or 30s., per knight. Some-times each baron had to argue with the King to find out how much money he would take instead of the knights. There were no clear rules about what the King ought to demand, and in 1215 this was precisely what the barons were determined to have.

Some baronial duties and royal rights had always left the King free to act almost as he wished. There was no precise rule settling the relief which barons had to pay; Robert de Ros, for example, had to pay a total of £1,000, John de Lacy over £4,500. There were no rules protecting the estates of wards in the King's hands; he or his men often taxed such lands heavily, sold grain and stock and did everything to get a quick profit before the ward came of age and got back the lands for himself. This was usually called 'wasting' an estate. Some of these things were done on John de Lacy's lands before he succeeded to them in 1213, for he was a minor when his father died in 1211.

The King used his rights of wardship as a way of making financial profits. In a similar way he used his rights to give widows and heiresses in marriage to increase the power of his officers and friends. For example, during the civil war in 1216, he married off Margaret, widow of Baldwin de Redvers, heir to the earldom of Devon, to his hated sheriff and military commander, Faulkes de Breauté. Sometimes, in contrast, he simply demanded heavy pay-ments from widows to preserve their widowhood and to obtain their dower lands and marriage portion. Hawise, countess of Aumale, for example, was forced to offer over

£3,500 in 1212 to remain a widow or marry a man of her own choice, and to have her lands. She was a great land-owner who held the lordships of Holderness and Skipton in Yorkshire. She had had three husbands already.

On all these points Magna Carta laid down strict rules. Henceforth the King was to ask for consent before he levied a scutage or aid, unless it was for the three purposes of *ransoming* himself if he were taken prisoner, or knighting his eldest son, or marrying his eldest daughter.

The relief which a baron had to pay was now fixed at £100. It was also stated that there was to be no 'wasting' of the lands of wards; when they came of age, they were to receive their lands fully stocked and in proper condition. Widows were now to have their *dowers* and *marriage portions* without charge or delay; they were not to be forced to marry again, but they still had to get the agreement of the King or their lord if they decided to do so on their own. Heiresses were no longer to be married to men of lower rank; before the King arranged a marriage for an heiress he was to tell her relatives.

These are just some of the benefits which the barons wished to get from Magna Carta. There were others to their advantage too, which were concerned, for example, with the payment of the barons' debts to the King or arranged for the return of estates, castles and hostages which the King had seized. But these which I have described were especially important because they made fixed rules about the way the King was to treat the barons. Most of these rules became part of the law of the land; this meant that in future if there was a dispute between king and barons, the barons could appeal to the law.

The barons were not the only men to benefit in this way from Magna Carta. Many of the regulations which were for them especially, were put at the beginning of the Charter.

But these regulations numbered less than twenty of the sixty-three sections in the Charter. The Church, the knights, the merchants and townspeople, and even the peasants, also gained something.

WHAT MAGNA CARTA SAID: 2. *For the Church*
Although the sections which concerned the barons appeared near the beginning of the Charter, the first section of all concerned the Church. This stated that the English Church was to be free and was to enjoy its rights and liberties without any hindrance. Elections to offices in the Church were to be made freely by the clergymen concerned, without any interference by the King. This last section simply repeated a promise which King John had made to the Church in a charter of November 1214, at the end of his quarrel with the Pope.

Apart from this section, Magna Carta had very little to say about the Church. It gave clergymen a few benefits here and there. Also, most of the bishops and some of the abbots held baronies of the King and owed him knight service and other baronial duties; they therefore benefited from some of these sections which benefited the barons. But the leading rebels of 1215 were mostly barons who did not bother very much about the rights of the Church. The clergy had already won their battle against King John when he had given in to Pope Innocent, in 1213 and 1214. Thus Magna Carta was not really concerned with the Church's problems.

The knights were a very different matter. They gained a great deal from Magna Carta.

Most of these men held their land of the great barons in return for similar services to those which the barons gave to the King. Also the barons enjoyed rights over the knights similar to those which the King had over them. The knights were the men whom the barons sent to the King when he demanded their customary military service. When the King took scutage from the barons, the barons took it, in turn, from the knights. The knights were bound by custom to give their lords aid in the form of money; they paid relief to their lords for their land; if the heir to a knight's estate was a minor, then he became a ward of his lord; widows and heirs of knights were only supposed to marry with their lords' consent.

On all these points the knights benefited from the promises which the barons forced out of the King, for Magna Carta stated that they would grant to their men what the King was granting to them. One section, that dealing with the King's right to a money aid, was repeated almost word for word so as to limit the barons' rights in this matter in the same way as the King's.

In addition to this, certain sections of Magna Carta were especially concerned with the knights. Just as the baron's relief was fixed at £100, so the relief of a knight was fixed at £5. King John had often charged knights very much more than this, although this had been the usual sum in the reign of his father.

Another section said that they were not to be forced to do more duties than they ought by custom to perform. King John had seized every opportunity to add to the duties of knights and had tried especially to get them to serve in lengthy campaigns in distant parts of France.

Some of these sections were important. That which fixed a knight's relief at £5, for example, became established law, and lawyers came to distinguish between a knight and a baron partly on the different reliefs which each paid.

The knights gained more from Magna Carta than any other class except the barons. They were second in importance only to the barons amongst the laymen of the time.

WHAT MAGNA CARTA SAID:

4. *For the Merchants and Townspeople*

King John had granted charters to many towns, giving them special privileges in governing themselves and in trading both within and without their town walls. Yet he was often unpopular with townspeople and merchants, and in 1215 the towns were divided, some supporting the King and some, including London, supporting the rebels.

Magna Carta contained some sections for the townspeople and merchants. The Londoners were specially favoured, for the King now promised that he would not force them to pay aids without their agreement. Hitherto John and earlier kings had taxed them whenever they wanted. No other town obtained this privilege, but Magna Carta confirmed those privileges which towns already held by charter.

One section in particular was important for merchants, especially for those who came from London. This section said that special kinds of *weirs* called *kiddles* were to be removed from the Thames, the Medway and other English rivers. These kiddles were barriers across the rivers in which nets were fixed to catch fish. They prevented ships from sailing up and down; this was a nuisance because, in those days of bad roads, many merchants used the rivers for trading. The Londoners had already paid £1,000 for two charters, one from King Richard and one from King John, which promised to destroy these weirs. But it took a long time to get such promises carried out in the Middle Ages. Even this clause in Magna Carta did not settle matters. In 1227 the Londoners bought yet another charter from Henry III confirming that weirs would be destroyed on the Thames and Medway. Even so, this clause in Magna Carta was important. It is still law, and can still be used if someone obstructs an English river by making a weir.

Other sections in Magna Carta were not aimed so much at pleasing English merchants as at improving trade. One section said that there was to be a single system of weights and measures throughout the country and that all woven cloth was to be two yards wide. This repeated earlier efforts which had been made under Richard and John to apply a general standard. Many merchants did not like it, especially those who liked to sell short measure! Sometimes, too, weavers could not produce cloth of the required width without altering their looms; they therefore had to make payments to be exempted from these rules.

Another section gave special protection to foreign merchants trading in England. King John had often seized them and their goods, and had taxed them very heavily. This was now forbidden. This meant that the foreign competitors of the English merchants were given a better chance of trading. The barons benefited from this more than the townspeople, for they liked to buy the luxuries which foreign merchants brought, especially wine, spices, furs and expensive clothing.

Magna Carta was granted to all free men in the kingdom. Only such peasants as were free men, therefore, could enjoy any of its privileges; in some counties such as Leicestershire, Nottinghamshire, Lincolnshire, Norfolk and Suffolk, there were a considerable number of these free peasants.

The most important sections of the Charter for these men were those which dealt with what we call *purveyance*. This meant that the King's officers seized goods for the King's needs, to supply his court as it travelled about the country, or to replenish the stocks of food in his castles. Magna Carta now said that the King's officials were not to take corn or other things in this way without paying for them They were not to seize horses and carts for carrying the King's goods unless the owners of the horses and carts agreed. Also they were not to force villagers to work at building bridges and keeping river banks in good repair except in cases where this was one of the usual duties of the villagers.

Some of these rules were made to protect the lords of the manor, for they too had corn and horses and carts. But the free peasants gained too. Those peasants who were not free men, however, got almost nothing out of Magna Carta, for they were not named among those to whom it was granted.

These men, the *bondsmen*, *serfs* or *villeins*, along with their families, formed the largest number of people in England. They were still treated as the property of the lords of the manor; their services could be given away or bought or sold. They are scarcely mentioned at all in Magna Carta and were really left out of it altogether.

Some writers have thought that Magna Carta was a very selfish piece of work, made by the barons for themselves and no one else. Certainly, Magna Carta was made to benefit the smaller part of the population, for it left out the bondsmen. However, although men saw a big difference between a bondsman and a free man, they did not draw any other sharp dividing line between different kinds of people. Barons and knights and merchants had different tasks to do and different positions and different privileges. But they were all free men, who were, in many matters, equal in the eyes of the law. In Magna Carta the term 'free man' is used to include them all from the baron down to the free peasant. Many of the most important sections of Magna Carta were made not for any one particular class but for all those who were free.

Everyone had suffered because the last three kings, Henry II, Richard and John, especially the last, had done all they could to squeeze more money out of England. They had expected their sheriffs and bailiffs to pay in each year more money to the Exchequer. These men, in turn, had had to get more money out of the people under their rule. So bitter were the complaints against them that John had found it necessary to sack some of them as far back as 1213, two years before Magna Carta. Some sheriffs received bribes; some imprisoned men without any real reason and held them until they paid a ransom; some seized lands which did not belong to them; some sat as judges in their own counties, thus preventing any complaint against them to the county court.

Magna Carta forbade all this. The King was no longer

to demand from his sheriffs more than the normal and customary *revenues* of their counties. Sheriffs and other bailiffs were not to act as judges. The King's officials were to be chosen only from those who knew the law of the land and were prepared to keep it. Twelve knights in each county were to enquire into how the sheriffs and bailiffs had behaved. Certain very unpopular sheriffs and bailiffs, all foreigners from Poitou, were mentioned by name and were to be dismissed from their posts.

WHAT MAGNA CARTA SAID: 8. *The Royal Forests*
The royal forests were especially unpopular in 1215. These were areas like Sherwood, in Nottinghamshire, or the New Forest, in Hampshire, or the Forest of Dean, in Gloucestershire, in which a special forest law was in force in addition to the common law. Most of them were heavily wooded areas, but they were not the King's sole property. Barons, knights and others often had their own woods within them. There were villages and manors within them too, in which peasants lived an ordinary country life,

Hunting deer

ploughing, sowing, reaping and pasturing their flocks. This map shows you how many such villages there were within the bounds of Sherwood Forest.

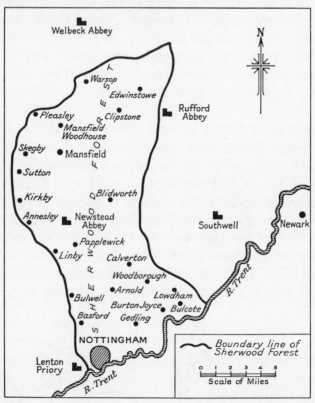

Welbeck Abbey

Warsop

Edwinstowe

Pleasley

Clipstone

Rufford Abbey

Mansfield Woodhouse

Skegby

Mansfield

Sutton

Kirkby

Blidworth

Annesley

Newstead Abbey

Southwell

Newark

Papplewick

Linby

Calverton

Woodborough

Arnold

Lowdham

Bulwell

Burton Joyce

Bulcote

Basford

Gedling

NOTTINGHAM

Lenton Priory

R. Trent

R. Trent

Boundary line of Sherwood Forest

0 1 2 3 4 5
Scale of Miles

The royal forest law aimed at preserving the beasts of the forest, especially the deer, and at preserving the woods in which they lived. It laid down very heavy punishments for poaching and forbade any improvement of land within the forest by clearing trees, enclosing land, digging ditches, or raising hedges or fences or buildings. King Henry II had added to the areas covered by the forest law.

62

Both he and King John tried to enforce the law very strictly, for they both loved hunting and both of them saw that they could get a great deal of money from the punishments they imposed on those who broke the law. In the civil war in 1215 the King's forests were one of the favourite targets for attack. The rebels joyfully chopped down the trees, probably in order to use the timber to strengthen their castles, and chased and killed the royal game.

Magna Carta tried to limit the King's forest rights. It stated that those areas which had been brought under the forest law by King John were to be placed outside it once more. It stated that those who lived outside the forest were not normally to be summoned before the justices of the forest who enforced the hated forest law. It arranged that those knights who were enquiring into the behaviour of sheriffs should also examine the bad features of the forest law so that they could be abolished.

WHAT MAGNA CARTA SAID: 9. *Law and Justice*
The most important sections of Magna Carta from which all free men benefited concerned the giving of justice. Hitherto kings had looked upon this as just another of their royal powers. Justice was theirs to give or withhold; they gave it freely and fairly to many men in many different kinds of case, but to others they sold it, for they looked at giving justice as an exercise of their own power for which they naturally expected payment. Such a man as William de Mowbray, as you saw on p. 24, had to pay heavily even to obtain a promise of fair treatment by King John. To others, John and his predecessors would not give justice either for love or money, for, as John once said, it was right and proper that a king should do justice

to and reward his friends, but not his enemies. Doing justice was still a very personal power. It became so personal in John's later years that more and more cases came to be heard before him, or the judges present with him, as the court travelled about the country. Judges no longer sat at Westminster to hear everyday actions. It became increasingly difficult to get a judgement, and when you did get one, the result often depended on whether you were the King's friend or his enemy. John even encouraged his barons to bring legal claims against each other in order to divide them, and hence to control them.

What Magna Carta aimed to do here was to separate justice from politics.

First, it laid down that ordinary actions between parties were to be dealt with by judges sitting at a fixed place.

Secondly, it laid down that money fines were to fit the crime and were not to be too large. The point of this was to prevent the King from imposing very heavy fines for small offences with the aim of *blackmailing* the victim into obedience and filling his own treasure-chests. John had often imposed very large fines. Turn back to pages 25 and 29 to see how he treated Thomas of Moulton and Robert de Ros, for example.

Thirdly, it laid down that the King was not to deny justice to anyone, or delay it or sell it. This expressed men's hopes that the royal courts and the King himself would do justice fairly.

Finally, Magna Carta tried to stop the King punishing his subjects by unlawful methods. Henceforth he was not to take action against them unless the law said he could. This was laid down in the most famous section of all in Magna Carta, chapter 39, in which the King was made to say—

No free man shall be seized or imprisoned or be deprived of his lands or outlawed or exiled or in any way ruined, nor shall we go against him, nor shall we send men against him unless by the lawful judgement of his peers[1] or by the law of the land.

In some ways this section was vague, but it was the first time in English history that the king had agreed that he could not do just what he liked with his subjects but only what the law allowed him to do. If this rule had been accepted in 1210, Matilda de Briouze would not have been starved to death; in 1215 men hoped that Magna Carta would put a stop to this kind of thing.

WHY MAGNA CARTA WAS IMPORTANT

You may think that the term 'free man' is not very clear, that, as applied to King John's time, it describes not one class but many, from baron down to peasant. You may think, too, that the last three sections I have described are vague. In this you are right. These sections were vague and did simply assert general rules or principles. But it is because of this that Magna Carta survived and that men turned to it, generation after generation, as a defence of what they considered were their rights.

Magna Carta was produced at a time when the King and his barons were the most important people in the political life of the country. But they lived in a world in which all free men counted for something and had their rights. It was a time, too, when men were beginning to consider questions like—What is justice? What is good

[1] See Glossary.

65

government?—as questions of principle, not just as matters affecting their own interests as individuals or as members of a class.

Hence in Magna Carta, among the many sections which concerned special interests and particular problems, there were other sections which stated good general rules for all time. Later generations often misunderstood what men thought and felt in 1215 and often forgot that the barons were fighting, before all else, for themselves. Men came to interpret some of these sections of Magna Carta in ways scarcely imagined by those who had won them from the King in 1215. In the fourteenth century, for example, men argued that the words 'the law of the land', in chapter 39 of Magna Carta, referred to trial by the established courts of common law. In 1215 many of these courts had not yet been set up. In the seventeenth century some thought that the 'judgement by peers' of chapter 39 meant trial by jury. They forgot that trial by jury was not yet established when Magna Carta was drawn up in 1215.

There are many other examples of this kind, some of them quite recent. Within the last ten years a lawyer has appealed to the section of Magna Carta which stated that widows were to have their dower and marriage portion without delay, in order to persuade the Ministry of Pensions to pay a widow's pension punctually. Needless to say, there were no widows' pensions in 1215. Similarly, in 1958 a lawyer argued that a section of the Charter which said that men could enter or leave the country without hindrance meant that our Government today should not require us to have passports when we go abroad.

In 1215 Magna Carta said nothing about trial by jury, or widows' pensions, or passports. But, in stating general principles of justice, the barons and King John produced a document which men could later re-interpret, as the times changed. The principles themselves have not been changed. It is as important in our own day as it was in 1215, that the Government should rule according to law, even though the Government now means the Prime Minister and the Cabinet instead of King John and his servants. Because it asserted this great principle, statesmen, lawyers and ordinary people, both in England and the United States of America, still meet to commemorate the granting of Magna Carta in June 1215.

The Civil War and After

In 1215 one section of Magna Carta was especially important. This came near the end of the document and said that the barons were to choose twenty-five of their number who were to see that Magna Carta was properly enforced. If anyone felt that its terms were not being obeyed, he could report the matter to any four of the twenty-five barons. If these four could not persuade the King to deal with the matter properly, then the twenty-five, or the majority of them, if they so decided, could force the King to do what was required by seizing his lands and castles. These twenty-five men were chosen at Runnymede. Twenty-four of them were barons or earls or the sons of barons or earls, and they included many of those whom I have mentioned, like Robert fitz Walter, William de Mowbray, John de Lacy, Robert de Ros, Roger Bigod, Richard of Clare and Robert de Vere. The twenty-fifth was the Mayor of London. These men together were to act as a court which would see that the King kept the promises he had made in Magna Carta.

The letters which Elias of Dereham and the other messengers carried into the countryside from Runnymede ordered that all free men in the land should swear an oath that they would obey the orders of these men and help them in forcing the King to do what was required. The barons had set themselves up as greater than the King. This court of twenty-five was to sit in judgement on the King in those cases where he refused to accept the claims of men who said that he had taken property from them unlawfully. Turn back to p. 46 and you will see that these cases included a claim to the custody of the Tower of London.

King John quickly decided that he would rather go to war than agree to all this baronial committee demanded. Arguments between him and the barons dragged on through July and August. Both the King and the barons were very suspicious of each other. Each side was busy fortifying castles. By the third week in July, at the very latest, John wrote to Pope Innocent and asked him to *annul* Magna Carta. But war broke out in September, even before the Pope's letter cancelling Magna Carta arrived in England. King John was never to reign in peace again.

THE CIVIL WAR

The war was not fought by the English alone. King John used hired troops from Poitou and Flanders, and he had to keep lines of communication open across the Channel. The rebel barons, too, found willing allies in King Alexander of Scotland, who claimed the three Border counties as his own, and in Prince Louis of France, whom they now put forward as King of England instead of John.

The war opened with a fight for the castles of Kent, for to control these was to command the main routes to the English Channel. Here John was successful. He already held Dover at the outbreak of war. The rebels seized Rochester Castle, but John immediately laid siege to it. He had mines dug under one of the angle towers and

Rochester Castle, showing the corner John mined

brought it down. When it was rebuilt after the war it was as a round tower, not a rectangular one, and so you can still tell which corner John attacked.

Rochester fell on November 26th. It was a great victory, and the King followed it up with a campaign in which he ravaged the lands of his enemies from the English Channel north up to and over the Scottish Border.

Despite this the two parties were fairly evenly balanced. King John was unable to prevent Prince Louis from landing in Kent in May 1216. Louis added to the strength of the rebels, for he brought his own army with him, and many who had been for King John so far, hastened to join the French prince.

Even so, William Marshal, Ranulf, Earl of Chester, and some others still stood by the King, and he still had his

Prince Louis's landing, by Matthew Paris

foreign captains and hired troops. At Dover, Hubert de Burgh, who had been the King's Chamberlain and was now the Chief Justiciar, continued to hold out bravely, despite Prince Louis' persistent attempts to take the castle. Right up to his death, which occurred at Newark in the night of October 18th, 1216, John fought on courageously and vigorously. He remained dangerous to the last. Towards the end he showed some repentance for his worst deeds, for he gave permission to one of William

Dover Castle today

71

Newark Castle, the gatehouse

de Briouze's daughters to found a religious house for the salvation of the souls of her father and of Matilda, his wife, and William, his eldest son. He also made a will in which he wisely put his son in the care of the Pope's agent in England and William Marshal and other loyal barons. His last expressed wish was to be buried at Worcester.

John's son Henry, who was now nine years old, was knighted and crowned at Gloucester on October 28th. Men quickly rallied to his cause and to the barons who supported him. Within a year two great victories had been won.

King John's tomb in Worcester Cathedral

Lincoln Castle in the eighteenth century

First, on May 20th, 1217, William Marshal, Ranulf of Chester and their men beat an army of rebels and Frenchmen who were laying siege to Lincoln Castle. They caught most of them in the narrow streets of the town beneath the castle and the cathedral and captured most of them. One important Frenchman, the Count of Perche, was killed. Here is Matthew Paris' drawing of the battle. He shows the Count of Perche's death and the flight of the few rebels who escaped.

A second important victory was won at sea off Sandwich on August 24th, 1217. In this fight the English fleet, watched from the shore by William Marshal, destroyed a large French fleet which was bringing reinforcements to Prince Louis. The English surprised the enemy by throwing pots of powdered lime at their ships so as to make their eyes smart and blind them for a time. Here is the end of the battle as drawn by Matthew Paris. You can see the English sailors shooting or slinging the pots of lime.

This defeat finally decided Prince Louis to make peace. He agreed to withdraw from England. King Henry's supporters agreed that the rebel barons should be restored to their lands as they had held them before the war. Detailed terms were settled in a conference held at Kingston-on-Thames on September 12th. By the end of the month Louis had sailed for France and most of the rebels had submitted.

Louis and Henry exchange the
the kiss of peace

74

There were three outstanding reasons for this sudden end to the war and for the young King Henry's success.

First, those who rebelled were inspired above all by a hatred of King John. Once he was dead, one of the causes of the war was removed.

Secondly, the Church, represented by the Pope's agent, or *Legate* as he was called, supported King John and his son throughout the war. The rebels and their foreign allies were excommunicated; the war against them and Prince Louis was made a holy war, a Crusade.

Finally, once King John was dead, William Marshal and other loyal barons were free to agree that many of the regulations of Magna Carta were just and reasonable. A new version of Magna Carta was made and sealed with the Earl Marshal's seal as early as November 12th, 1216, within less than a month of King John's death. This repeated many of the sections of the original version of 1215, but left out several sections of it which were 'grave and doubtful' and required further consideration. These sections included those, for example, on scutages and aids, on freedom to travel in and out of the country, and on the baronial committee of twenty-five.

One of the terms of the Treaty of Kingston was that King Henry would restore the liberties which had been demanded from King John, and soon afterwards in 1217 yet a third version of Magna Carta was made. This repeated many of the more important sections of the 1215 version, such as those which concerned law and justice and those which concerned reliefs and wardship. William Marshal and his friends thought that some of the sections of the 1215 version were unwise and went too far in putting limits on what the King could do. The section

75

concerning the twenty-five barons was now omitted, and so were those concerning scutages and aids. Also, certain sections, like those which ordered the restoration of land and hostages which King John had seized, were now out of date. They too were not included in the new version.

However, the new version also contained some new sections which had not been in the original Magna Carta of 1215. Most important of all, the matters concerning the royal forests were put in a separate Charter of the Forest which was made at London on November 6th, 1217. This softened the cruelty and harshness of the existing forest law and made arrangements which placed many areas outside the bounds of the forest. Henceforth Magna Carta and the Charter of the Forest went together. When one was confirmed in later years, so usually was the other.

Although they had been beaten in battle, therefore, the rebels achieved a great deal, for the peace agreed in 1217 partly gave them what they wanted. Much of what they had demanded from John was now granted by his son. The Charters issued in 1217 were issued yet again in 1225, this time with a few unimportant changes in the wording. This version of Magna Carta became part of the law of the land.

By this time men were already appealing to Magna Carta and the Charter of the Forest to defend what they considered to be their rights against the King and his officials. In later years they frequently demanded that the Charters should be reissued and publicly confirmed when they considered that the King's government was too oppressive. In 1253 the Archbishop of Canterbury pronounced a sentence of *excommunication* against all those who did not keep the Charters. This sentence was confirmed by the Pope in 1254. Events had moved fast since Pope Innocent annulled the first Magna Carta in 1215.

Men quickly came to remember what Magna Carta contained. In 1215 the King's sheriffs had been ordered to have the original version read out aloud in public. A confirmation of the Charters in 1265 provided for a public reading twice a year in the county courts at Easter and Michaelmas. In 1279 the Archbishop of Canterbury tried to arrange for copies to be posted up in a prominent place in all cathedrals and other important churches. In 1297 it was ordered that the Charters should be read publicly twice yearly in all cathedrals. In 1300 the Charters were to be read four times annually before the people in full meetings of the county courts. By 1301 Magna Carta had been reissued or publicly confirmed by King John's son, Henry III, or by his grandson, Edward I, on at least fifteen occasions. Men did not let go of what their ancestors had first won in 1215.

HOW DO WE KNOW?

In telling this story I have used two main kinds of information: the narratives of monastic chroniclers and other writers, and the records of King John's government.

1. THE NARRATIVE SOURCES

Many different *annals* or *chronicles* were written in different monasteries during or shortly after John's time. The three most important of these come from Coggeshall in Essex, St. Albans in Hertfordshire and probably from Barnwell, near Cambridge. This last one is not so hard on John as the others. The St. Albans one is the most hostile to the King and also tells the longest and most exciting story. It was written by one of the St. Albans monks called Roger of Wendover, who was Prior of a religious house at Belvoir during the civil war. It is to Roger that we owe the stories of the baronial meetings at St. Paul's, London, in 1213 and at the abbey of Bury St. Edmunds in 1214.

Roger wrote this part of his chronicle sometime after 1225 and probably before 1230. It was later rewritten by another St. Albans monk, Matthew Paris, who probably died in 1259. Matthew wrote other important works, too. The stories of Robert fitz Walter and Binham Priory and of Faulkes de Breauté's dream are taken from his *Deeds of the Abbots of St. Albans*.

There are two other important narrative sources which were written not in Latin but in French. One was written by a man who came over with John's Flemish allies to help him in the civil war. It is called the *History of the Dukes of Normandy and the Kings of England* and it gives perhaps the best account of all of the civil war. The other is a very long poem about William Marshal. This gives us the story of William playing jackstraw with King Stephen and many other details of his life. One of William Marshal's own servants must have told these stories to the writer of the poem and so we know much more about him than any of the other barons.

What we know about the rest comes largely from records; partly from the records they themselves left when they granted land to a monastic house, or arranged a marriage, for example; but mainly from the records of the King's government.

2. THE RECORDS OF KING JOHN'S GOVERNMENT

King John's reign is the first for which we have a reasonably complete set of documentary records. There are three kinds.

First, there are long *parchment* rolls, made up of pieces of parchment attached to each other head to foot, on which the clerks of the Chancery copied most of the letters and charters they wrote and sent out for the King. These record, for example, grants of land, letters to sheriffs about all kinds of things connected with the government of the realm, and letters ordering payments from the Treasury. Except for a few years for which the rolls are lost, they give us a continuous account of the King's government and on the way he treated barons, knights, church-men and merchants. The letter about the imprisonment of Thomas de Moulton, for example, comes from these rolls. Not every document was copied on to the rolls. Magna Carta, for example, was not entered on the Charter Roll. But most documents were.

Secondly, there are the records of the Exchequer and the King's household which deal with money. The most important of these was the roll on which, each year, the clerks of the *Treasurer* wrote the annual account of the King's revenues. This was called the Pipe Roll or the Great Roll of the Pipe, getting this name from the shape of the parchment skins when they were rolled up. The Pipe Rolls can tell us about the moneys due to the King from the sheriffs, about the money fines taken by the King's justices, and about the fines and other debts which the barons owed to the King.

They also tell us how the King spent his money. There is more about this on the expense rolls of the Household. From these we know what sort of cloth the King bought for his own use and even how often he took a bath. This was about once every three weeks, which was probably fairly frequently by the standards of cleanliness of his day.

Finally, there are the records of the justice done in the King's court and the rolls of his justices who travelled about the country hearing cases as they went. These tell us a great deal about how the courts of justice worked, about the punishment of criminals and about quarrels between individual people. The case between William de Mowbray and William de Stuteville and that between Robert fitz Walter and the monks of St. Albans and Binham appear in these records. So also do those cases where King John showed mercy and understanding.

3. THE DRAWINGS

Many of the pictures in this book are taken from drawings done by Matthew Paris in the margins of his chronicles. He was one of the greatest artists of medieval England. You may already have seen his famous picture of an elephant.

Some of his pictures are entirely imaginary. For example, he drew at least two pictures of Rochester Castle. The two shown below are not very much alike. Neither of them is an accurate drawing of Rochester, as you can see if you turn to p. 70. You can also compare his drawing of Lincoln castle on p. 73 with a later picture of the castle on the same page.

Although his pictures are not very truthful in matters like this, they are very useful in other ways. For example, they give a very good idea of the dress and armour of the early thirteenth century. You can see that they come very close to the way men are dressed in effigies and on seals.

But the pictures are valuable in themselves as vigorous, skilful and sometimes beautiful drawings. One of Matthew's best drawings is of himself. Here he is, pictured in adoration at the feet of the Virgin and Child.

WHY MEDIEVAL PEOPLE USED SEALS

Have you noticed that King John did not sign Magna Carta but sealed it? Today when we write an important document, like a will, we sign it with our full signature in order to make it quite plain that we agree with what the document says and intend to keep the promises we make in it or expect other people to keep them. We each have our own special way of writing our own name which we call our *signature*. It is very important that we should have a distinctive way of writing our signature so that it is not easy to copy (or *forge*). A forged document is one which pretends to be written and signed by one person or group of people but is really done by another person or group. You can easily think out why people should want to forge documents.

The problem for medieval people was that most of them could not sign their names, so how could kings and lords make it plain that they had agreed to what a charter or document said and meant to keep their promises? In order that other people should know that the document was not a forgery, they had to have a very distinct way of marking it. So they sealed it with their own distinct and special seal which stood instead of a signature.

Each great man—king, bishop, baron or knight—had his own seal with his own distinctive design upon it. A baron's seal usually showed him in armour on horseback as you can see if you turn to p. 26. Sometimes it showed his special emblem. Some seals had two faces and showed both.

The seal was made in a matrix or mould in which these designs were cut on the inside face or faces of a hollow case. A tongue was cut from the parchment of the charter or letter which was to be sealed, or sometimes a strip of parchment or a piece of cord was threaded through a slit or hole in the bottom of the document. Soft wax was put round this and then pressed into the mould so that the designs came out on the wax. When the wax set the seal was safely fastened to the document. Sometimes in museums you can still see these documents with the seals hanging from the bottom. Look out for them.

Today it is a crime to forge someone else's signature. In the Middle Ages it was most important to see that a lord's seal was not stolen and used to seal a document he would not agree with, perhaps making promises he would not want to keep. So most lords gave their seals to very trusted servants to guard. The keeper of the seal must not put his lord's seal to any document without being told by his lord to do so. The Kings of England each had a special Great Seal which was used on all important documents, such as charters. It was kept by the Chancellor who was supposed not to seal any charter except by the king's command. Sometimes the king had a little seal (or private or privy seal) as well, generally used to seal less important documents like letters.

Magna Carta was solemnly sealed with the Great Seal. Now you know why it is wrong to say (as many people do), 'King John signed Magna Carta'.

THINGS TO DO

ABOUT MAGNA CARTA

1. Try to visit one of the places where you can see one of the copies of Magna Carta.

2. Try to visit Runnymede where there is a memorial to Magna Carta and a museum.

3. Draw a picture of the meeting between the King and barons at Runnymede, *or* act the scene at Runnymede.

4. Write a letter from a bishop to his cathedral clergy telling of the events at Runnymede.

5. Find out from newspapers how men discuss and settle important matters today, at international conferences, for example, or in disputes between employers and trade unions.

Discuss how the methods of settling disputes have changed since 1215.

6. Find out about other famous documents such as:
   (*a*) The Petition of Right of 1628.
   (*b*) The Declaration of Rights of 1689.
   (*c*) The Declaration and Resolves of the first Continental Congress of America, 1774
   (*d*) The United Nations Declaration of Human Rights of 1948.
In what ways are they like Magna Carta? In what ways do they differ from Magna Carta?

7. Find out what Magna Carta says about rivers and forests. Why were rivers and forests more important in 1215 than now?

ABOUT KING JOHN

1. Try to go to Worcester to see his tomb or visit one of the places where he stayed frequently.

2. Compose a letter from a baron to his family telling of a visit of the King to the local county town and of the things he did there.

3. Hold a trial of King John. Have a counsel for the prosecution and a counsel for the defence. Let the rebels be witnesses for the prosecution and the loyal barons and other supporters of the King witnesses for the defence. Don't forget to cross-examine the witnesses. Don't forget to let John say something in his own defence.

4. Find out and read some of the stories and plays in which John appears, especially the following:

(*a*) William Shakespeare's play *King John*.

(*b*) Sir Walter Scott's *Ivanhoe*.

(*c*) J. D. Edgar, *Runnymede and Lincoln Fair*.

5. Do you think that the above books give a good picture of what John was like or not?

ABOUT THE BARONS

1. Find out and read the songs which the barons would listen to in their halls and the stories they would know. These include:

(*a*) *The Song of Roland*,

(*b*) the tales of King Arthur and his knights.

2. Write the best stories you can find in these of:

(*a*) men who were specially loyal and chivalrous,

(*b*) men who betrayed their lord and were guilty of treason.

3. Compare the characters of Charlemagne or King Arthur as they appear in these stories with that of King John.

ABOUT THE REBELLION AGAINST KING JOHN

1. Use your atlases to find the places where the rebel barons whom I have mentioned held their chief estates.

2. Draw a map and put these places on it. Also put in those places which were important in the civil war.

3. In which parts of the country was the rebellion centred?

ABOUT CASTLES

1. Is there a castle in your neighbourhood which was built by the time of King John? Try to visit it.

2. Draw a picture of it and make a model of it. Draw a plan of it showing the keep, the outer walls and the gatehouse.

3. Find out about the occasions when the castle was attacked.

GLOSSARY

alms: charitable gifts, usually to the poor.

ancestor, ancestress: one's parents, grand-parents, and so on.

annals: narrative of events year by year.

annul: to cancel or abolish.

bailiff: administrative officer put in charge of his office or district by a superior, e.g. by the king. Often a *sheriff's* assistant.

ballad: poem or song, written in a simple rhyming style, usually telling of the adventures of a popular hero.

baron: important vassal, usually of the King and normally holding his land by knight service.

barony: large estate or number of estates held by a baron.

to blackmail: to hold a threat over someone.

bondsman, villein or serf: dependent peasant who was bound to his lord and who occupied his land usually on condition of labouring on his lord's estates.

brutality: cruelty.

Chancellor: head of the King's writing office, the Chancery, in charge of all his secretarial work and of the Great Seal.

charter: written document recording a grant of rights of any kind, e.g. land or privileges, by one person or persons to others.

chronicle: narrative arranged in order of time.

constable: commander, usually of a castle, sometimes of an army.

dower: that portion of her husband's land which a widow continued to hold after her husband's death.

effigy: portrait or image; especially a figure, usually carved in some kind of stone, lying prone on top of a tomb.

Exchequer: chief department of the court concerned with the receipt and account of the money due to the King. Its work was directed by the Treasurer and the Barons of the Exchequer.

to excommunicate: to cut off someone from the sacraments of the Church and from communion with the Church.

to forge: to write a document or *signature* in order to pass it off as written by someone else.

heir: a person, usually a descendant, to whom lands, property and title pass on the death of the owner.

homage: public act recognizing dependence on and superiority of a lord.

hostage: person surrendered as a pledge of loyalty and good behaviour.

hue and cry: public outcry for the pursuit of a criminal and the public pursuit of such a person.

to inherit: to obtain land, property and title as an *heir*.

Interdict: suspension of the normal functions of the Church.

justiciar: Judge or justice. Chief Justiciar, the chief judicial and administrative officer of the kingdom, especially important when the King was absent abroad.

keep: chief stronghold of a castle.

kiddle: weir or barrier across a river or stream made for the purpose of catching fish.

Legate: clergyman instructed by the Pope to represent him.

marches: borderlands between two countries, especially between England and Wales and England and Scotland.

marriage portion: portion given to a bride at her marriage.

matrix: mould in which material is cast or shaped.

oath: statement in which there is an appeal to God to witness its truth, or, in the case of a promise, to witness that it will be carried out.

parchment: skin of an animal, specially prepared so that it can be written on; usually the skin of a sheep.

peer: one who is equal in standing; one's equal before the law.

purveyance: right to collect foodstuffs and requisition transport for the King's use, if on payment, at prices fixed by the King's men.

ransom: sum paid by a prisoner to buy his freedom; also to pay such a sum.

relief: money paid by an heir for admission to his inheritance.

revenues: regular income.

to scoff: to jeer at somebody or something.

scutage: payment in money instead of doing knight service, assessed at so much per knight.

seal: engraved stamp of metal used to make an impression in wax, or the wax bearing this impression.

serf: see *bondsman*.

sheriff: administrative officer (reeve) in charge of a county (shire): a shire reeve.

signature: person's name written in his own hand.

spigurnel: officer of the Chancery whose job it was to seal documents. The origin of this curious name is not known.

squire: attendant on a knight, often one who was preparing to become a knight himself.

steward: person who manages an estate on behalf of a lord or employer.

Treasurer: see *Exchequer*.

treaty: written agreement between equals, often one between different countries.

vassal: dependent of a lord.

villein: see *bondsman*.

ward: minor (under the age of twenty-one) in the care of a guardian.

weir: dam across a river which raises its level and over which it flows.